AF575372

DEALING WITH
A MOVE
SAMANTHA S. BELL
KITCHE
childsworld.com

Published by The Child's World®
800-599-READ • www.childsworld.com

Photography Credits
Photographs ©: iStockphoto, cover, 1, 14, 22; Monkey Business Images/iStockphoto, 5; Shutterstock Images, 6, 17, 19, 20; Red Line Editorial, 9; Odua Images/Shutterstock Images, 11; J. Bryson/iStockphoto, 12–13

ISBN Information
9781503885400 (Reinforced Library Binding)
9781503885554 (Portable Document Format)
9781503886193 (Online Multi-user eBook)
9781503886834 (Electronic Publication)

LCCN 2023937458

Printed in the United States of America

Samantha S. Bell has written more than 150 nonfiction books for children. She lives in the foothills of the Blue Ridge Mountains with her family and lots of cats. With four children of her own, she knows that sometimes even the youngest kids have to work through tough situations.

TABLE OF CONTENTS

CHAPTER 1

When a Move Happens

People move for many different reasons. Sometimes they need more or less space for their family. They might find a new place to live in the same area. But sometimes people move to a different city. They might need to move because a parent has a new job. Some people move to be closer to other family members, such as grandparents. They might move for a change in **lifestyle**. For example, they may move from a large, busy city to a small, quiet town.

Many people use trucks to move their belongings.

Packing for a move can be tiring. It can make people sad, too.

Sometimes families move so the children can go to a certain school.

Moving can be both exciting and stressful. Sometimes moving to a new home and neighborhood can seem like an adventure. Some people buy decorations or furniture for their new home. If the move is to a different city, there will be new places to visit and things to see.

Moving can also be hard. People must pack up all their belongings. If a family owns their home, they will probably try to sell it. If someone is leaving the area, he or she may say goodbye to people in the community. This can include neighbors, teachers, coaches, and librarians.

Leaving behind friends can also be hard. People may feel very sad, especially if they are close with their friends. They will miss spending time together. Some people may feel angry about having to leave their friends. They may also be worried about making new friends.

Sometimes people are nervous about going to a new school. They do not know the teachers. They may take new classes or learn different things, too. They may be nervous about finding their way around the school. They may be worried about being the new kid in class.

Moving to a new place might be the next step for a family. But it may not be an easy one. There are many strong feelings that come with a move. It may take some time to feel at home in a new place.

Why Do People Move?

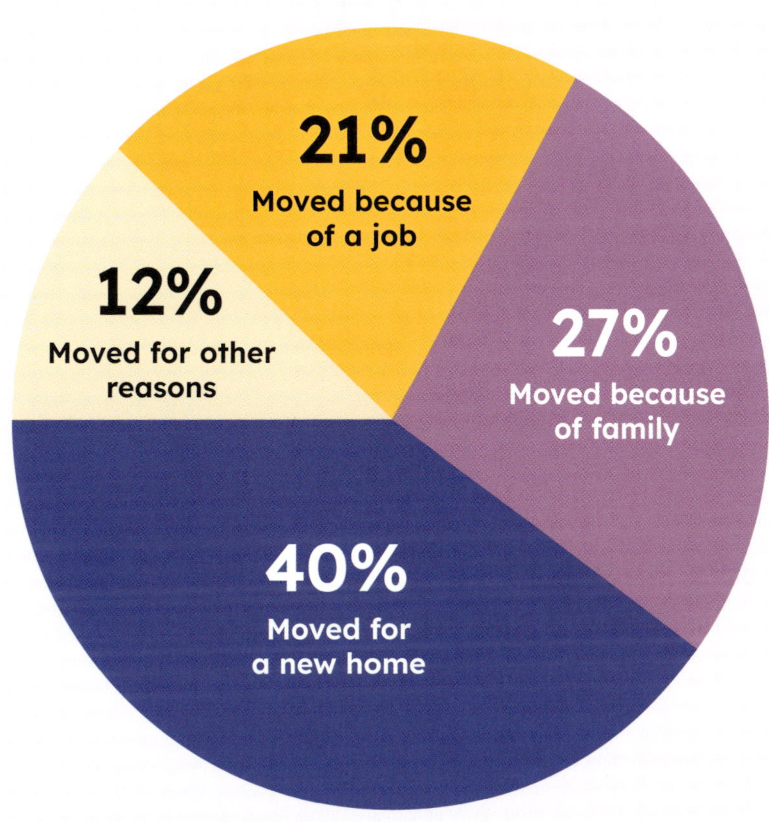

Much of the time, people move because they need a different home. But people also move because of their jobs or families.

CHAPTER 2

Coping with a Move

A move is a big change. But there are things people can do to make it easier. They can find out about the new location before moving there. That way, they may feel less **anxious**. They can find out where the grocery store, the park, and the library are. They can find out what clubs, sports, and other activities are available.

People can explore their new neighborhood by going for a walk.

Students can visit their new school before they go to class. This may help starting school feel less scary. They can find important places such as the office, cafeteria, classrooms, and bathrooms. This may help students feel better on their first day.

After moving to a new place, it is important to keep old **routines** as much as possible. For example, people should try to keep the same mealtimes and bedtimes. Routines give people a sense of control. This helps reduce stress.

After moving, people can get involved in the community right away. They can join clubs or sports teams. Public libraries often have free activities for people of all ages. Getting involved can help people meet new friends. They can start to build a community near their new home.

People may meet their neighbors at library events.

Video calls are a good way to stay in touch.

Moving with the Military

Families in the military often have to move every two or three years. Military members must move for training or new jobs. Moving so often can be hard. Unpacking and setting up the new home right away can help. Having familiar objects and foods around can make people feel better.

Staying in touch with old friends also makes a move easier. People can write letters or send postcards. They can text or email old friends. They can talk over video calls. Many people play video games together online, too.

Sometimes people have negative feelings about moving. They might feel angry, sad, or stressed. It's important to talk to someone about these emotions. A parent or a **counselor** can help. Sometimes, adults may just listen. Other times, they may suggest ideas to help the person feel better.

CHAPTER 3

Helping a Friend Deal with a Move

When a friend is moving away, there are things a person can do to help make the move easier. One of the best things a person can do is offer **comfort**. The friend may be feeling many difficult emotions. He or she may be confused, angry, or sad. Writing the friend a letter can help. People could also make a list of all the things the friend can do in the new city. Just listening to the friend talk about the move is another way to comfort him or her.

Talking to a friend can help people feel better.

People can organize a going-away party for a friend who is moving far away. A party gives everyone a chance to show how much they care. It will also give the friend time to say goodbye.

Some people create a **scrapbook** for their friend. It might include **mementos** from activities they did together. These could be ticket stubs, photos, or receipts. Letters and drawings can also be included. People may give the scrapbook to the friend at the going-away party or right before he or she leaves. A framed photo is another gift that could help a friend who is moving away.

Friends can look through their scrapbook together.

Helping a New Student

Sometimes there is a new student in class. Most likely, the student feels nervous and alone. Other students can help by talking to her. They might give her tips about school activities. They can sit with her at lunch. They can help make those first days in the new school easier.

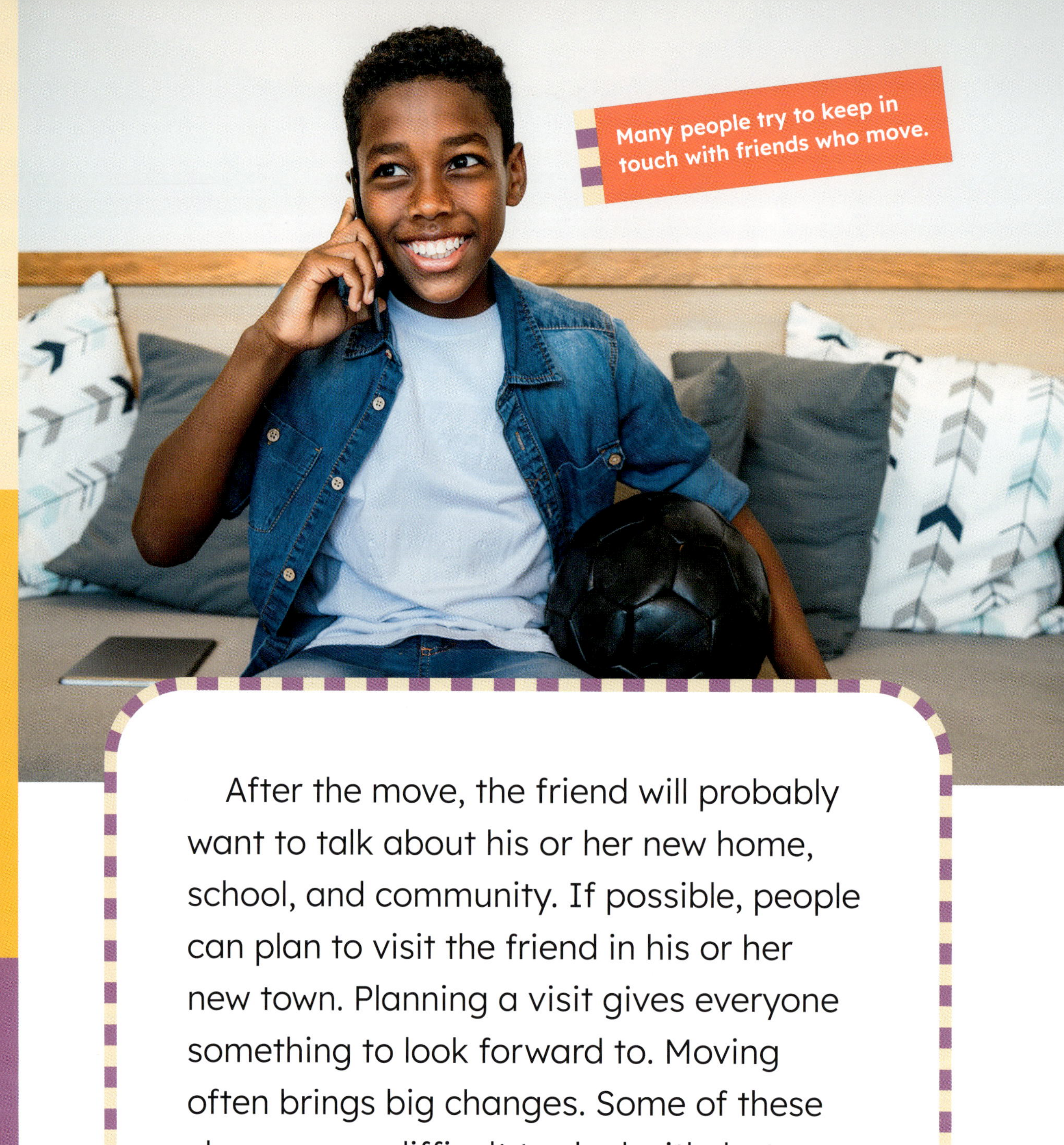

Many people try to keep in touch with friends who move.

After the move, the friend will probably want to talk about his or her new home, school, and community. If possible, people can plan to visit the friend in his or her new town. Planning a visit gives everyone something to look forward to. Moving often brings big changes. Some of these changes are difficult to deal with, but others can be fun and exciting.

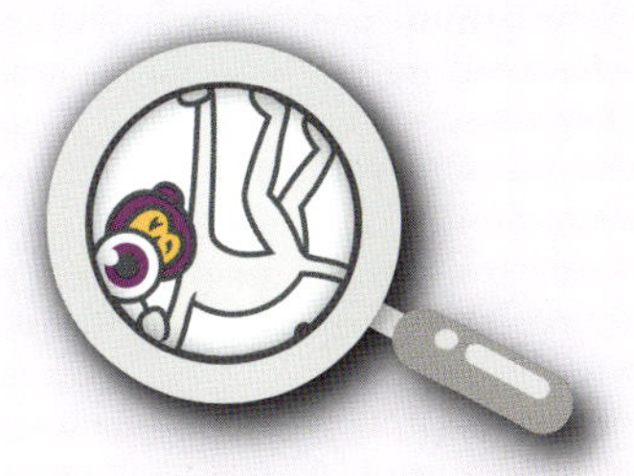

Wonder More

Wondering about New Information

How much did you know about moving before reading this book? What new information did you learn? Write down three new facts that this book taught you. Did the new information surprise you? Why or why not?

Wondering How It Matters

Have you ever moved to a new home? If so, how does the information in this book relate to your life? If not, imagine how other kids who have moved may feel. What impact might this have had on their lives?

Wondering Why

When a friend moves away, he or she may try to stay in touch with the people he or she left behind. How do you think staying in touch helps the person who moved?

Ways to Keep Wondering

Moving to a different place may bring up lots of different feelings, all at the same time. After reading this book, what questions do you have about moving to a new home? What can you do to learn more about how to cope during a move?

Fast Facts

- There are many reasons people might move. They may move to live in a bigger or smaller home. Others move because of a parent's job or to be closer to family.
- Moving can be exciting and stressful at the same time. It may bring up some difficult feelings. People may feel angry, scared, nervous, or sad.
- Learning about the new town and school can help people get ready for the move.
- Staying in touch with old friends can make the move easier.
- If a friend is moving, people can say goodbye to the friend with a going-away party, a special card, or a gift.

Glossary

anxious (ANGK-shuhs) Anxious means to feel worried or nervous about something uncertain. Moving can make people feel anxious.

comfort (KUM-furt) To offer comfort means to help someone feel better. Being a good listener can give a friend comfort.

counselor (KOWN-suh-lur) A counselor is a person who helps people work through strong feelings. Talking to a counselor after moving can help someone feel better.

lifestyle (LIFE-styl) A person's lifestyle is the way that he or she lives. Someone might move to a small town to have a more relaxed lifestyle.

mementos (muh-MEN-tohz) Mementos are objects that remind someone of a person or event. Mementos remind friends of each other.

routines (roo-TEENZ) Routines are sets of things that people do regularly. One of the family's routines was eating dinner at 7 p.m. every night.

scrapbook (SKRAP-buk) A scrapbook is a book with blank pages for saving photos, letters, and other mementos. A person might give her friend a scrapbook before the friend moves.

Find Out More

In the Library

Allen, Vanessa Green. *Me and My Feelings: A Kids' Guide to Understanding and Expressing Themselves*. Emeryville, CA: Rockridge Press, 2019.

Lindeen, Mary. *A New Home*. Chicago, IL: Norwood House Press, 2022.

Petersen, Christine. *The Smart Kid's Guide to Moving*. Parker, CO: The Child's World, 2015.

On the Web

Visit our website for links about dealing with a move:
childsworld.com/links

Note to Parents, Caregivers, Teachers, and Librarians: We routinely verify our Web links to make sure they are safe and active sites. So encourage your readers to check them out!

Index